MW00899644

THIS BOOK IS THE

_____

Complete Running Diary
52 Week Training Log
Sebastian Elliott

There are a lot of web sites and apps for runners. Living in a multiple FitBit household, I know this all too well. These computerized options are great, but they lack the tangibility of a book such as this. Nothing can replace the excitement and pride of holding a completed, physical runner's log book in your hands.

It might be a bit tattered and worse for wear, but you can wrap your hands around it and feel the weight knowing that it represents hours of the joys and pains of your running life. You can flip through it and see your own handwriting reminding you of your commitment and your accomplishments.

I take full advantage of computerized measurement and analysis, but I also keep a physical log and suggest that you do, too. It's a very personal and positive experience that mirrors the personal and positive experience you have when running. *Sebastian*

FastForwardPublishing.com

ISBN-13: 978-1507752432
ISBN-10: 1507752431

Table of Contents

Introduction

"Why run? I run because I am an animal. I run because it is part of my genetic wiring. I run because millions of years of evolution have left me programmed to run. And finally, I run because there's no better way to see the sun rise and set... What the years have shown me is that running clarifies the thinking process as well as purifies the body. I think best – most broadly and most fully – when I am running."

Amby Burfoot

One of the most important activities a runner can do is keep a log. Why? Here are 12 quick reasons -- and with a little thought you might come up with half-a-dozen more!

1. **Satisfaction.** When you record a run, it reinforces what you have accomplished.

2. **Motivation.** Running is hard work and it's tough to maintain a high level of motivation. Reviewing your training diary reinforces the investment you have made in the journey to reach your goals.

3. **Pride.** Unlike other activities like painting or woodworking, when you are a runner, you can't see or touch our accomplishments. By recording your runs, all that mileage and achievement is at your fingertips and easy to relive.

4. **Enhanced Performance.** By taking a look at your training log, you can see the cause and effect of your runs over time. Should you increase or decrease your mileage? Do you need more or less speed work. By looking at your workouts over time, you can find ways to train more effectively.

5. **New Shoes.** You should be changing shoes every 300-400 miles. Your log shows you when replacements are in order.

6. **Fixes.** If you have a bad race or an injury, the information in your log can show you how to fix it. Perhaps you have better race performance when the week prior to the race follows a particular pattern or maybe you discover that you tend to get injured in specific circumstances (e.g., increasing weekly mileage above a certain percentage or doing too many miles on hills).

7. **Confidence.** After keeping a running log for a while, flip through the pages you have filled out and see how much hard work you have completed, what you have accomplished and how you've progressed.

8. **Communication.** Share your running diary with a friend, running partner or coach for feedback and or motivation.

9. **Accountability.** A review of your running log reminds you of the standards you have set for yourself as a runner and encourages you to live up to those standards.

10. **Racing.** Log your race results and then compare them to similar races. Also compare those results to your pre-race training. By measuring and comparing race information you will know if you are improving, stalled, or slowing down and make decisions on moving forward to the next race.

11. **Answers.** If you find yourself particularly tired, you can check back in your diary and see if you have had a big jump in mileage or if you have been steadily increasing for too long or find possible answers to a number of different important questions.

12. **Self-Awareness.** Because you are unique, you won't necessarily respond exactly the same was as another runner to a particular training program. Reviewing the data in your log will help you tailor a program that is fine-tuned to you.

"People sometimes sneer at those who run every day,
claiming they'll go to any length to live longer.
But don't think that's the reason most people run.
Most runners run not because they want to live longer,
but because they want to live life to the fullest.
If you're going to while away the years,
it's far better to live them with clear goals
and fully alive then in a fog,
and I believe running
helps you to do that.
Exerting yourself to the fullest
within your individual limits:
that's the essence of running,
and a metaphor for life…"

Haruki Murakami

Week of ___/___/_____ - ___/___/_____

Goals for Week: _____

_____

_____

MONDAY	Weather	Time	Distance	Weekly Total
Route:				
Cross Training:				
How I Felt:				

TUESDAY	Weather	Time	Distance	Weekly Total
Route:				
Cross Training:				
How I Felt:				

WEDNESDAY	Weather	Time	Distance	Weekly Total
Route:				
Cross Training:				
How I Felt:				

THURSDAY	Weather	Time	Distance	Weekly Total

Route:
Cross Training:
How I Felt:

FRIDAY	Weather	Time	Distance	Weekly Total

Route:
Cross Training:
How I Felt:

SATURDAY	Weather	Time	Distance	Weekly Total

Route:
Cross Training:
How I Felt:

SUNDAY	Weather	Time	Distance	Weekly Total

Route:
Cross Training:
How I Felt:

Week 1 Wrap Up

Did I meet my goals for the week?   ☐ Yes   ☐ No

What helped me reach my goals or what kept me from reaching my goals:

_____

_____

_____

How do I feel about that? _____

_____

_____

What will I change next week? _____

_____

_____

What will I not change next week? _____

_____

_____

Notes/Other Observations: _____

_____

_____

_____

_____

Total Miles to Date This Year: _____

"Running is my private time, my therapy, my religion."

Gail W. Kislevitz

Week of ___/___/_____ - ___/___/_____

Goals for Week: _____

_____

_____

MONDAY	Weather	Time	Distance	Weekly Total
Route:				
Cross Training:				
How I Felt:				

TUESDAY	Weather	Time	Distance	Weekly Total
Route:				
Cross Training:				
How I Felt:				

WEDNESDAY	Weather	Time	Distance	Weekly Total
Route:				
Cross Training:				
How I Felt:				

THURSDAY	Weather	Time	Distance	Weekly Total

Route:

Cross Training:

How I Felt:

FRIDAY	Weather	Time	Distance	Weekly Total

Route:

Cross Training:

How I Felt:

SATURDAY	Weather	Time	Distance	Weekly Total

Route:

Cross Training:

How I Felt:

SUNDAY	Weather	Time	Distance	Weekly Total

Route:

Cross Training:

How I Felt:

Week 2 Wrap Up

Did I meet my goals for the week?   ☐ Yes   ☐ No

What helped me reach my goals or what kept me from reaching my goals:

_____

_____

_____

How do I feel about that? _____

_____

_____

What will I change next week? _____

_____

_____

What will I not change next week? _____

_____

_____

Notes/Other Observations: _____

_____

_____

_____

_____

Total Miles to Date This Year: _____

"Running! If there's any activity happier, more exhilarating, more nourishing to the imagination, I can't think of what it might be. In running the mind flees with the body, the mysterious efflorescence of language seems to pulse in the brain, in rhythm with our feet and the swinging of our arms."

Joyce Carol Oates

Week of ___/___/_____ - ___/___/_____

Goals for Week: _____

_____

_____

MONDAY	Weather	Time	Distance	Weekly Total
Route:				
Cross Training:				
How I Felt:				

TUESDAY	Weather	Time	Distance	Weekly Total
Route:				
Cross Training:				
How I Felt:				

WEDNESDAY	Weather	Time	Distance	Weekly Total
Route:				
Cross Training:				
How I Felt:				

THURSDAY	Weather	Time	Distance	Weekly Total
Route:				
Cross Training:				
How I Felt:				

FRIDAY	Weather	Time	Distance	Weekly Total
Route:				
Cross Training:				
How I Felt:				

SATURDAY	Weather	Time	Distance	Weekly Total
Route:				
Cross Training:				
How I Felt:				

SUNDAY	Weather	Time	Distance	Weekly Total
Route:				
Cross Training:				
How I Felt:				

Week 3 Wrap Up

Did I meet my goals for the week?   ☐ Yes   ☐ No

What helped me reach my goals or what kept me from reaching my goals:

_____

_____

_____

How do I feel about that? _____

_____

_____

What will I change next week? _____

_____

_____

What will I not change next week? _____

_____

_____

Notes/Other Observations: _____

_____

_____

_____

_____

Total Miles to Date This Year: _____

The white space on this page is suitable for notes if needed.

"The biggest mistake that new runners make is that they tend to think in mile increments-1 mile, 2 miles, 3 miles. Beginning runners need to think in minutes, not miles."

Budd Coates

Week of ___/___/_____ - ___/___/_____

Goals for Week: _____

_____

_____

MONDAY	Weather	Time	Distance	Weekly Total
Route:				
Cross Training:				
How I Felt:				

TUESDAY	Weather	Time	Distance	Weekly Total
Route:				
Cross Training:				
How I Felt:				

WEDNESDAY	Weather	Time	Distance	Weekly Total
Route:				
Cross Training:				
How I Felt:				

THURSDAY	Weather	Time	Distance	Weekly Total

Route:

Cross Training:

How I Felt:

FRIDAY	Weather	Time	Distance	Weekly Total

Route:

Cross Training:

How I Felt:

SATURDAY	Weather	Time	Distance	Weekly Total

Route:

Cross Training:

How I Felt:

SUNDAY	Weather	Time	Distance	Weekly Total

Route:

Cross Training:

How I Felt:

Week 4 Wrap Up

Did I meet my goals for the week?   □ Yes   □ No

What helped me reach my goals or what kept me from reaching my goals:

_____

_____

_____

How do I feel about that? _____

_____

_____

What will I change next week? _____

_____

_____

What will I not change next week? _____

_____

_____

Notes/Other Observations: _____

_____

_____

_____

_____

Total Miles to Date This Year: _____

The white space on this page is suitable for notes if needed.

"My whole teaching in one sentence is: "Run slowly, run daily, drink moderately, and don't eat like a pig."

Dr. Ernst van Aaken

Week of ___/___/_____ - ___/___/_____

Goals for Week: _____

_____

_____

MONDAY	Weather	Time	Distance	Weekly Total
Route:				
Cross Training:				
How I Felt:				

TUESDAY	Weather	Time	Distance	Weekly Total
Route:				
Cross Training:				
How I Felt:				

WEDNESDAY	Weather	Time	Distance	Weekly Total
Route:				
Cross Training:				
How I Felt:				

THURSDAY	Weather	Time	Distance	Weekly Total

Route:

Cross Training:

How I Felt:

FRIDAY	Weather	Time	Distance	Weekly Total

Route:

Cross Training:

How I Felt:

SATURDAY	Weather	Time	Distance	Weekly Total

Route:

Cross Training:

How I Felt:

SUNDAY	Weather	Time	Distance	Weekly Total

Route:

Cross Training:

How I Felt:

Week 5 Wrap Up

Did I meet my goals for the week?   ☐ Yes   ☐ No

What helped me reach my goals or what kept me from reaching my goals:

_____

_____

_____

How do I feel about that? _____

_____

_____

What will I change next week? _____

_____

_____

What will I not change next week? _____

_____

_____

Notes/Other Observations: _____

_____

_____

_____

_____

Total Miles to Date This Year: _____

"If you run, you are a runner. It doesn't matter how fast or how far. It doesn't matter if today is your first day or if you've been running for twenty years. There is no test to pass, no license to earn, no membership card to get. You just run."

John Bingham

Week of ___/___/_____ - ___/___/_____

Goals for Week: _____

_____

_____

MONDAY	Weather	Time	Distance	Weekly Total
Route:				
Cross Training:				
How I Felt:				

TUESDAY	Weather	Time	Distance	Weekly Total
Route:				
Cross Training:				
How I Felt:				

WEDNESDAY	Weather	Time	Distance	Weekly Total
Route:				
Cross Training:				
How I Felt:				

THURSDAY	Weather	Time	Distance	Weekly Total

Route:

Cross Training:

How I Felt:

FRIDAY	Weather	Time	Distance	Weekly Total

Route:

Cross Training:

How I Felt:

SATURDAY	Weather	Time	Distance	Weekly Total

Route:

Cross Training:

How I Felt:

SUNDAY	Weather	Time	Distance	Weekly Total

Route:

Cross Training:

How I Felt:

Week 6 Wrap Up

Did I meet my goals for the week?   ☐ Yes   ☐ No

What helped me reach my goals or what kept me from reaching my goals:

_____

_____

_____

How do I feel about that? _____

_____

_____

What will I change next week? _____

_____

_____

What will I not change next week? _____

_____

_____

Notes/Other Observations: _____

_____

_____

_____

_____

Total Miles to Date This Year: _____

*"If you have a bad workout or run a bad race,
allow yourself exactly 1 hour to stew about it --
then move on."*

Steve Scott

Week of ___/___/_____ - ___/___/_____

Goals for Week: _____

_____

_____

MONDAY	Weather	Time	Distance	Weekly Total
Route:				
Cross Training:				
How I Felt:				

TUESDAY	Weather	Time	Distance	Weekly Total
Route:				
Cross Training:				
How I Felt:				

WEDNESDAY	Weather	Time	Distance	Weekly Total
Route:				
Cross Training:				
How I Felt:				

THURSDAY	Weather	Time	Distance	Weekly Total
Route:				
Cross Training:				
How I Felt:				

FRIDAY	Weather	Time	Distance	Weekly Total
Route:				
Cross Training:				
How I Felt:				

SATURDAY	Weather	Time	Distance	Weekly Total
Route:				
Cross Training:				
How I Felt:				

SUNDAY	Weather	Time	Distance	Weekly Total
Route:				
Cross Training:				
How I Felt:				

Week 7 Wrap Up

Did I meet my goals for the week?   ☐ Yes   ☐ No

What helped me reach my goals or what kept me from reaching my goals:

_____

_____

_____

How do I feel about that? _____

_____

_____

What will I change next week? _____

_____

_____

What will I not change next week? _____

_____

_____

Notes/Other Observations: _____

_____

_____

_____

_____

Total Miles to Date This Year: _____

*"Occasionally pick up speed-for 2 minutes, tops –
then settle back into your former pace. Sometimes
this is all you need to snap out of a mental and
physical funk. Pick a downhill stretch if you can,
and really lengthen your stride."*

Mark Plaatjes

Week of ___/___/_____ - ___/___/_____

Goals for Week: _____

_____

_____

MONDAY	Weather	Time	Distance	Weekly Total
Route:				
Cross Training:				
How I Felt:				

TUESDAY	Weather	Time	Distance	Weekly Total
Route:				
Cross Training:				
How I Felt:				

WEDNESDAY	Weather	Time	Distance	Weekly Total
Route:				
Cross Training:				
How I Felt:				

THURSDAY	Weather	Time	Distance	Weekly Total
Route:				
Cross Training:				
How I Felt:				

FRIDAY	Weather	Time	Distance	Weekly Total
Route:				
Cross Training:				
How I Felt:				

SATURDAY	Weather	Time	Distance	Weekly Total
Route:				
Cross Training:				
How I Felt:				

SUNDAY	Weather	Time	Distance	Weekly Total
Route:				
Cross Training:				
How I Felt:				

Week 8 Wrap Up

Did I meet my goals for the week?   ☐ Yes   ☐ No

What helped me reach my goals or what kept me from reaching my goals:

_____

_____

_____

How do I feel about that? _____

_____

_____

What will I change next week? _____

_____

_____

What will I not change next week? _____

_____

_____

Notes/Other Observations: _____

_____

_____

_____

_____

Total Miles to Date This Year: _____

The white space on this page is suitable for notes if needed.

> *"When it's pouring rain and you're bowling along*
> *through the wet, there's satisfaction in knowing*
> *you're out there and the others aren't."*
>
> **Peter Snell**

Week of ___/___/_____ - ___/___/_____

Goals for Week: _____

_____

_____

MONDAY	Weather	Time	Distance	Weekly Total
Route:				
Cross Training:				
How I Felt:				

TUESDAY	Weather	Time	Distance	Weekly Total
Route:				
Cross Training:				
How I Felt:				

WEDNESDAY	Weather	Time	Distance	Weekly Total
Route:				
Cross Training:				
How I Felt:				

THURSDAY	Weather	Time	Distance	Weekly Total

Route:

Cross Training:

How I Felt:

FRIDAY	Weather	Time	Distance	Weekly Total

Route:

Cross Training:

How I Felt:

SATURDAY	Weather	Time	Distance	Weekly Total

Route:

Cross Training:

How I Felt:

SUNDAY	Weather	Time	Distance	Weekly Total

Route:

Cross Training:

How I Felt:

Week 9 Wrap Up

Did I meet my goals for the week?   ☐ Yes   ☐ No

What helped me reach my goals or what kept me from reaching my goals:

_____

_____

_____

How do I feel about that? _____

_____

_____

What will I change next week? _____

_____

_____

What will I not change next week? _____

_____

_____

Notes/Other Observations: _____

_____

_____

_____

Total Miles to Date This Year: _____

"For me, running is a lifestyle and an art. I'm far more interested in the magic of it than the mechanics."

Lorraine Moller

Week of ___/___/_____ - ___/___/_____

Goals for Week: _____

_____

_____

MONDAY	Weather	Time	Distance	Weekly Total

Route:
Cross Training:
How I Felt:

TUESDAY	Weather	Time	Distance	Weekly Total

Route:
Cross Training:
How I Felt:

WEDNESDAY	Weather	Time	Distance	Weekly Total

Route:
Cross Training:
How I Felt:

THURSDAY	Weather	Time	Distance	Weekly Total

Route:

Cross Training:

How I Felt:

FRIDAY	Weather	Time	Distance	Weekly Total

Route:

Cross Training:

How I Felt:

SATURDAY	Weather	Time	Distance	Weekly Total

Route:

Cross Training:

How I Felt:

SUNDAY	Weather	Time	Distance	Weekly Total

Route:

Cross Training:

How I Felt:

Week 10 Wrap Up

Did I meet my goals for the week?   ☐ Yes   ☐ No

What helped me reach my goals or what kept me from reaching my goals:

_____

_____

_____

How do I feel about that? _____

_____

_____

What will I change next week? _____

_____

_____

What will I not change next week? _____

_____

_____

Notes/Other Observations: _____

_____

_____

_____

_____

Total Miles to Date This Year: _____

"Running hills breaks up your rhythm and forces
your muscles to adapt to new stresses.
The result? You become stronger."

Eamonn Coghlan

Week of ___/___/_____ - ___/___/_____

Goals for Week: _____

_____

_____

MONDAY	Weather	Time	Distance	Weekly Total
Route:				
Cross Training:				
How I Felt:				

TUESDAY	Weather	Time	Distance	Weekly Total
Route:				
Cross Training:				
How I Felt:				

WEDNESDAY	Weather	Time	Distance	Weekly Total
Route:				
Cross Training:				
How I Felt:				

THURSDAY	Weather	Time	Distance	Weekly Total

Route:

Cross Training:

How I Felt:

FRIDAY	Weather	Time	Distance	Weekly Total

Route:

Cross Training:

How I Felt:

SATURDAY	Weather	Time	Distance	Weekly Total

Route:

Cross Training:

How I Felt:

SUNDAY	Weather	Time	Distance	Weekly Total

Route:

Cross Training:

How I Felt:

Week 11 Wrap Up

Did I meet my goals for the week?   ☐ Yes   ☐ No

What helped me reach my goals or what kept me from reaching my goals:

_____

_____

_____

How do I feel about that? _____

_____

_____

What will I change next week? _____

_____

_____

What will I not change next week? _____

_____

_____

Notes/Other Observations: _____

_____

_____

_____

_____

Total Miles to Date This Year: _____

The white space on this page is suitable for notes if needed.

> *"If 15 minutes is all the time I have, I still run.*
> *Fifteen minutes of running is better than*
> *not running at all."*
>
> **Dr. Duncan Macdonald**

Week of ___/___/_____ - ___/___/_____

Goals for Week: _____

_____

_____

MONDAY	Weather	Time	Distance	Weekly Total
Route:				
Cross Training:				
How I Felt:				

TUESDAY	Weather	Time	Distance	Weekly Total
Route:				
Cross Training:				
How I Felt:				

WEDNESDAY	Weather	Time	Distance	Weekly Total
Route:				
Cross Training:				
How I Felt:				

THURSDAY	Weather	Time	Distance	Weekly Total

Route:

Cross Training:

How I Felt:

FRIDAY	Weather	Time	Distance	Weekly Total

Route:

Cross Training:

How I Felt:

SATURDAY	Weather	Time	Distance	Weekly Total

Route:

Cross Training:

How I Felt:

SUNDAY	Weather	Time	Distance	Weekly Total

Route:

Cross Training:

How I Felt:

Week 12 Wrap Up

Did I meet my goals for the week?   ☐ Yes   ☐ No

What helped me reach my goals or what kept me from reaching my goals:

_____

_____

_____

How do I feel about that? _____

_____

_____

What will I change next week? _____

_____

_____

What will I not change next week? _____

_____

_____

Notes/Other Observations: _____

_____

_____

_____

_____

Well Done! You've Completed a 3 Full Months.   **Total Miles to Date This Year:** _____

"If there's one thing we runners do, it's endure.
We endure through long runs and hard workouts,
weeks of bad weather, and days of low energy.
We do what it takes to see things through to the end.
We can achieve amazing things in the rest of our lives
by practicing that virtue in our non-running endeavors."

Scott Douglas

Week of ___/___/_____ - ___/___/_____

Goals for Week: _____

_____

_____

MONDAY	Weather	Time	Distance	Weekly Total
Route:				
Cross Training:				
How I Felt:				

TUESDAY	Weather	Time	Distance	Weekly Total
Route:				
Cross Training:				
How I Felt:				

WEDNESDAY	Weather	Time	Distance	Weekly Total
Route:				
Cross Training:				
How I Felt:				

THURSDAY	Weather	Time	Distance	Weekly Total
THURSDAY				
Route:				
Cross Training:				
How I Felt:				

FRIDAY	Weather	Time	Distance	Weekly Total
FRIDAY				
Route:				
Cross Training:				
How I Felt:				

SATURDAY	Weather	Time	Distance	Weekly Total
SATURDAY				
Route:				
Cross Training:				
How I Felt:				

SUNDAY	Weather	Time	Distance	Weekly Total
SUNDAY				
Route:				
Cross Training:				
How I Felt:				

Week 13 Wrap Up

Did I meet my goals for the week?   ☐ Yes   ☐ No

What helped me reach my goals or what kept me from reaching my goals:

_____

_____

_____

How do I feel about that? _____

_____

_____

What will I change next week? _____

_____

_____

What will I not change next week? _____

_____

_____

Notes/Other Observations: _____

_____

_____

_____

_____

Total Miles to Date This Year: _____

*"Run with your heart instead of your mind. When you
run with your mind, you think of the things
you can and can't do. But when you run with
your heart you forget about what you can't do,
and you just go out and do it."*

Gerry Lindgren

Week of ___/___/_____ - ___/___/_____

Goals for Week: _____

_____

_____

MONDAY	Weather	Time	Distance	Weekly Total
Route:				
Cross Training:				
How I Felt:				

TUESDAY	Weather	Time	Distance	Weekly Total
Route:				
Cross Training:				
How I Felt:				

WEDNESDAY	Weather	Time	Distance	Weekly Total
Route:				
Cross Training:				
How I Felt:				

THURSDAY	Weather	Time	Distance	Weekly Total

Route:

Cross Training:

How I Felt:

FRIDAY	Weather	Time	Distance	Weekly Total

Route:

Cross Training:

How I Felt:

SATURDAY	Weather	Time	Distance	Weekly Total

Route:

Cross Training:

How I Felt:

SUNDAY	Weather	Time	Distance	Weekly Total

Route:

Cross Training:

How I Felt:

Week 14 Wrap Up

Did I meet my goals for the week?   □ Yes   □ No

What helped me reach my goals or what kept me from reaching my goals:

_____

_____

_____

How do I feel about that? _____

_____

_____

What will I change next week? _____

_____

_____

What will I not change next week? _____

_____

_____

Notes/Other Observations: _____

_____

_____

_____

_____

Total Miles to Date This Year: _____

"Noontime running provides a triple benefit: daylight, a break from the workday, and a chance to avoid eating a heavy lunch."

Joe Henderson

Week of ___/___/_____ - ___/___/_____

Goals for Week: _____

_____

_____

	Weather	Time	Distance	Weekly Total
MONDAY				
Route:				
Cross Training:				
How I Felt:				

	Weather	Time	Distance	Weekly Total
TUESDAY				
Route:				
Cross Training:				
How I Felt:				

	Weather	Time	Distance	Weekly Total
WEDNESDAY				
Route:				
Cross Training:				
How I Felt:				

THURSDAY	Weather	Time	Distance	Weekly Total
Route:				
Cross Training:				
How I Felt:				

FRIDAY	Weather	Time	Distance	Weekly Total
Route:				
Cross Training:				
How I Felt:				

SATURDAY	Weather	Time	Distance	Weekly Total
Route:				
Cross Training:				
How I Felt:				

SUNDAY	Weather	Time	Distance	Weekly Total
Route:				
Cross Training:				
How I Felt:				

Week 15 Wrap Up

Did I meet my goals for the week?   ☐ Yes   ☐ No

What helped me reach my goals or what kept me from reaching my goals:

_____

_____

_____

How do I feel about that? _____

_____

_____

What will I change next week? _____

_____

_____

What will I not change next week? _____

_____

_____

Notes/Other Observations: _____

_____

_____

_____

_____

Total Miles to Date This Year: _____

"I believe in the runner's high, and I believe that those who are passionate about running are the ones who experience it to the fullest degree possible. To me, the runner's high is a sensational reaction to a great run! It's an exhilarating feeling of satisfaction and achievement. It's like being on top of the world, and truthfully there's nothing else quite like it!"

Sasha Azevedo

Week of ___/ ___/ _____ - ___/ ___/ _____

Goals for Week: _____

_____

_____

MONDAY	Weather	Time	Distance	Weekly Total
Route:				
Cross Training:				
How I Felt:				

TUESDAY	Weather	Time	Distance	Weekly Total
Route:				
Cross Training:				
How I Felt:				

WEDNESDAY	Weather	Time	Distance	Weekly Total
Route:				
Cross Training:				
How I Felt:				

THURSDAY	Weather	Time	Distance	Weekly Total

Route:

Cross Training:

How I Felt:

FRIDAY	Weather	Time	Distance	Weekly Total

Route:

Cross Training:

How I Felt:

SATURDAY	Weather	Time	Distance	Weekly Total

Route:

Cross Training:

How I Felt:

SUNDAY	Weather	Time	Distance	Weekly Total

Route:

Cross Training:

How I Felt:

Week 16 Wrap Up

Did I meet my goals for the week? □ Yes   □ No

What helped me reach my goals or what kept me from reaching my goals:

_____

_____

_____

How do I feel about that? _____

_____

_____

What will I change next week? _____

_____

_____

What will I not change next week? _____

_____

_____

Notes/Other Observations: _____

_____

_____

_____

_____

Total Miles to Date This Year: _____

The white space on this page is suitable for notes if needed.

"Some people train knowing they're not working as hard as other people. I can't fathom how they think."

Alberto Salazar

Week of ___/___/_____ - ___/___/_____

Goals for Week: _____

_____

_____

MONDAY	Weather	Time	Distance	Weekly Total
Route:				
Cross Training:				
How I Felt:				

TUESDAY	Weather	Time	Distance	Weekly Total
Route:				
Cross Training:				
How I Felt:				

WEDNESDAY	Weather	Time	Distance	Weekly Total
Route:				
Cross Training:				
How I Felt:				

THURSDAY	Weather	Time	Distance	Weekly Total

Route:

Cross Training:

How I Felt:

FRIDAY	Weather	Time	Distance	Weekly Total

Route:

Cross Training:

How I Felt:

SATURDAY	Weather	Time	Distance	Weekly Total

Route:

Cross Training:

How I Felt:

SUNDAY	Weather	Time	Distance	Weekly Total

Route:

Cross Training:

How I Felt:

Week 17 Wrap Up

Did I meet my goals for the week?   ☐ Yes   ☐ No

What helped me reach my goals or what kept me from reaching my goals:

_____

_____

_____

How do I feel about that? _____

_____

_____

What will I change next week? _____

_____

_____

What will I not change next week? _____

_____

_____

Notes/Other Observations: _____

_____

_____

_____

_____

Total Miles to Date This Year: _____

> *"Any idiot can train himself into the ground; the trick is doing the training that makes you gradually stronger."*
>
> **Keith Brantly**

Week of ___/___/_____ - ___/___/_____

Goals for Week: _____

_____

_____

MONDAY	Weather	Time	Distance	Weekly Total
Route:				
Cross Training:				
How I Felt:				

TUESDAY	Weather	Time	Distance	Weekly Total
Route:				
Cross Training:				
How I Felt:				

WEDNESDAY	Weather	Time	Distance	Weekly Total
Route:				
Cross Training:				
How I Felt:				

THURSDAY	Weather	Time	Distance	Weekly Total

Route:

Cross Training:

How I Felt:

FRIDAY	Weather	Time	Distance	Weekly Total

Route:

Cross Training:

How I Felt:

SATURDAY	Weather	Time	Distance	Weekly Total

Route:

Cross Training:

How I Felt:

SUNDAY	Weather	Time	Distance	Weekly Total

Route:

Cross Training:

How I Felt:

Week 18 Wrap Up

Did I meet my goals for the week?   ☐ Yes   ☐ No

What helped me reach my goals or what kept me from reaching my goals:

_____

_____

_____

How do I feel about that? _____

_____

_____

What will I change next week? _____

_____

_____

What will I not change next week? _____

_____

_____

Notes/Other Observations: _____

_____

_____

_____

_____

Total Miles to Date This Year: _____

"You can't climb up to the second floor without a ladder. When you set your goal too high and don't fulfill it, your enthusiasm turns to bitterness. Try for a goal that's reasonable, and then gradually raise it."

Emil Zatopek

Week of ___/___/_____ - ___/___/_____

Goals for Week: _____

_____

_____

MONDAY	Weather	Time	Distance	Weekly Total
Route:				
Cross Training:				
How I Felt:				

TUESDAY	Weather	Time	Distance	Weekly Total
Route:				
Cross Training:				
How I Felt:				

WEDNESDAY	Weather	Time	Distance	Weekly Total
Route:				
Cross Training:				
How I Felt:				

THURSDAY	Weather	Time	Distance	Weekly Total

Route:
Cross Training:
How I Felt:

FRIDAY	Weather	Time	Distance	Weekly Total

Route:
Cross Training:
How I Felt:

SATURDAY	Weather	Time	Distance	Weekly Total

Route:
Cross Training:
How I Felt:

SUNDAY	Weather	Time	Distance	Weekly Total

Route:
Cross Training:
How I Felt:

Week 19 Wrap Up

Did I meet my goals for the week?   □ Yes   □ No

What helped me reach my goals or what kept me from reaching my goals:

_____

_____

_____

How do I feel about that? _____

_____

_____

What will I change next week? _____

_____

_____

What will I not change next week? _____

_____

_____

Notes/Other Observations: _____

_____

_____

_____

_____

Total Miles to Date This Year: _____

*"Running is a road to self-awareness and reliance –
you can push yourself to extremes and learn the harsh
reality of your physical and mental limitations or
coast quietly down a solitary path watching
the earth spin beneath your feet."*

Doris Brown Heritage

Week of ___/ ___/ _____ - ___/ ___/ _____

Goals for Week: _____

_____

_____

MONDAY	Weather	Time	Distance	Weekly Total
Route:				
Cross Training:				
How I Felt:				

TUESDAY	Weather	Time	Distance	Weekly Total
Route:				
Cross Training:				
How I Felt:				

WEDNESDAY	Weather	Time	Distance	Weekly Total
Route:				
Cross Training:				
How I Felt:				

THURSDAY	Weather	Time	Distance	Weekly Total

Route:

Cross Training:

How I Felt:

FRIDAY	Weather	Time	Distance	Weekly Total

Route:

Cross Training:

How I Felt:

SATURDAY	Weather	Time	Distance	Weekly Total

Route:

Cross Training:

How I Felt:

SUNDAY	Weather	Time	Distance	Weekly Total

Route:

Cross Training:

How I Felt:

Week 20 Wrap Up

Did I meet my goals for the week?   ☐ Yes   ☐ No

What helped me reach my goals or what kept me from reaching my goals:

_____

_____

_____

How do I feel about that? _____

_____

_____

What will I change next week? _____

_____

_____

What will I not change next week? _____

_____

_____

Notes/Other Observations: _____

_____

_____

_____

_____

Total Miles to Date This Year: _____

"That's the thing about running: your greatest runs are rarely measured by racing success. They are moments in time when running allows you to see how wonderful your life is."

Kara Goucher

Week of ___/___/_____ - ___/___/_____

Goals for Week: _____

_____

_____

	Weather	Time	Distance	Weekly Total
MONDAY				
Route:				
Cross Training:				
How I Felt:				

	Weather	Time	Distance	Weekly Total
TUESDAY				
Route:				
Cross Training:				
How I Felt:				

	Weather	Time	Distance	Weekly Total
WEDNESDAY				
Route:				
Cross Training:				
How I Felt:				

THURSDAY	Weather	Time	Distance	Weekly Total

Route:

Cross Training:

How I Felt:

FRIDAY	Weather	Time	Distance	Weekly Total

Route:

Cross Training:

How I Felt:

SATURDAY	Weather	Time	Distance	Weekly Total

Route:

Cross Training:

How I Felt:

SUNDAY	Weather	Time	Distance	Weekly Total

Route:

Cross Training:

How I Felt:

Week 21 Wrap Up

Did I meet my goals for the week?　☐ Yes　　☐ No

What helped me reach my goals or what kept me from reaching my goals:

_____

_____

_____

How do I feel about that? _____

_____

_____

What will I change next week? _____

_____

_____

What will I not change next week? _____

_____

_____

Notes/Other Observations: _____

_____

_____

_____

_____

Total Miles to Date This Year: _____

The white space on this page is suitable for notes if needed.

"Never put a time limit on success... Success and gains start immediately and continue infinitely—you just get better and better. It is not a light switch; it is a dimmer switch—you just keep getting the light brighter and brighter."

Eric Orton

Week of ___/___/_____ - ___/___/_____

Goals for Week: _____

_____

_____

	Weather	Time	Distance	Weekly Total
MONDAY				

Route:

Cross Training:

How I Felt:

	Weather	Time	Distance	Weekly Total
TUESDAY				

Route:

Cross Training:

How I Felt:

	Weather	Time	Distance	Weekly Total
WEDNESDAY				

Route:

Cross Training:

How I Felt:

THURSDAY	Weather	Time	Distance	Weekly Total
Route:				
Cross Training:				
How I Felt:				

FRIDAY	Weather	Time	Distance	Weekly Total
Route:				
Cross Training:				
How I Felt:				

SATURDAY	Weather	Time	Distance	Weekly Total
Route:				
Cross Training:				
How I Felt:				

SUNDAY	Weather	Time	Distance	Weekly Total
Route:				
Cross Training:				
How I Felt:				

Week 22 Wrap Up

Did I meet my goals for the week?   ☐ Yes   ☐ No

What helped me reach my goals or what kept me from reaching my goals:

_____

_____

_____

How do I feel about that? _____

_____

_____

What will I change next week? _____

_____

_____

What will I not change next week? _____

_____

_____

Notes/Other Observations: _____

_____

_____

_____

_____

Total Miles to Date This Year: _____

The white space on this page is suitable for notes if needed.

"It may seem odd to hear a coach say this, but I think a really great training partner is more important than a coach."

Joan Nesbit

Week of ___/___/_____ - ___/___/_____

Goals for Week: _____

_____

_____

MONDAY	Weather	Time	Distance	Weekly Total
Route:				
Cross Training:				
How I Felt:				

TUESDAY	Weather	Time	Distance	Weekly Total
Route:				
Cross Training:				
How I Felt:				

WEDNESDAY	Weather	Time	Distance	Weekly Total
Route:				
Cross Training:				
How I Felt:				

THURSDAY	Weather	Time	Distance	Weekly Total

Route:

Cross Training:

How I Felt:

FRIDAY	Weather	Time	Distance	Weekly Total

Route:

Cross Training:

How I Felt:

SATURDAY	Weather	Time	Distance	Weekly Total

Route:

Cross Training:

How I Felt:

SUNDAY	Weather	Time	Distance	Weekly Total

Route:

Cross Training:

How I Felt:

Week 23 Wrap Up

Did I meet my goals for the week?   ☐ Yes   ☐ No

What helped me reach my goals or what kept me from reaching my goals:

_____

_____

_____

How do I feel about that? _____

_____

_____

What will I change next week? _____

_____

_____

What will I not change next week? _____

_____

_____

Notes/Other Observations: _____

_____

_____

_____

_____

Total Miles to Date This Year: _____

"Hydrate. Hydrate. Hydrate! In cold weather and warm. We use water to sweat, lubricate joints, tendons, and ligaments, and to carry blood efficiently to major organs. I work all day at hydrating."

Dr. Alex Ratelle

Week of ___/___/_____ - ___/___/_____

Goals for Week: _____

_____

_____

MONDAY	Weather	Time	Distance	Weekly Total
Route:				
Cross Training:				
How I Felt:				

TUESDAY	Weather	Time	Distance	Weekly Total
Route:				
Cross Training:				
How I Felt:				

WEDNESDAY	Weather	Time	Distance	Weekly Total
Route:				
Cross Training:				
How I Felt:				

THURSDAY	Weather	Time	Distance	Weekly Total

Route:

Cross Training:

How I Felt:

FRIDAY	Weather	Time	Distance	Weekly Total

Route:

Cross Training:

How I Felt:

SATURDAY	Weather	Time	Distance	Weekly Total

Route:

Cross Training:

How I Felt:

SUNDAY	Weather	Time	Distance	Weekly Total

Route:

Cross Training:

How I Felt:

Week 24 Wrap Up

Did I meet my goals for the week?　☐ Yes　　☐ No

What helped me reach my goals or what kept me from reaching my goals:

_____

_____

_____

How do I feel about that? _____

_____

_____

What will I change next week? _____

_____

_____

What will I not change next week? _____

_____

_____

Notes/Other Observations: _____

_____

_____

_____

_____

Total Miles to Date This Year: _____

"The benefits and opportunities of running are available to anyone. You don't have to be born a natural athlete, and you don't have to be uniquely gifted. A life-shaping experience is there for the taking, waiting right outside your door."

Donald Buraglio

Week of __/__/_____ - __/__/_____

Goals for Week: _____

_____

_____

MONDAY	Weather	Time	Distance	Weekly Total
Route:				
Cross Training:				
How I Felt:				

TUESDAY	Weather	Time	Distance	Weekly Total
Route:				
Cross Training:				
How I Felt:				

WEDNESDAY	Weather	Time	Distance	Weekly Total
Route:				
Cross Training:				
How I Felt:				

THURSDAY	Weather	Time	Distance	Weekly Total

Route:
Cross Training:
How I Felt:

FRIDAY	Weather	Time	Distance	Weekly Total

Route:
Cross Training:
How I Felt:

SATURDAY	Weather	Time	Distance	Weekly Total

Route:
Cross Training:
How I Felt:

SUNDAY	Weather	Time	Distance	Weekly Total

Route:
Cross Training:
How I Felt:

Week 25 Wrap Up

Did I meet my goals for the week?   ☐ Yes   ☐ No

What helped me reach my goals or what kept me from reaching my goals:

_____

_____

_____

How do I feel about that? _____

_____

_____

What will I change next week? _____

_____

_____

What will I not change next week? _____

_____

_____

Notes/Other Observations: _____

_____

_____

_____

_____

Total Miles to Date This Year: _____

The white space on this page is suitable for notes if needed.

*"Running is real and relatively simple — but it ain't easy.
It's a challenge. It takes work. It takes commitment.
You have to get out of bed, get out the door, down the street.
You have to risk getting cold, wet, or too hot. Maybe whack
some over-zealous hound on the snout — or 'Hot Rod Harry'
on the hood — every now and again. And, of course,
you have to take your very first run."*

Mark Will-Weber

Week of ___/___/_____ - ___/___/_____

Goals for Week: _____

_____

_____

	Weather	Time	Distance	Weekly Total
MONDAY				
Route:				
Cross Training:				
How I Felt:				

	Weather	Time	Distance	Weekly Total
TUESDAY				
Route:				
Cross Training:				
How I Felt:				

	Weather	Time	Distance	Weekly Total
WEDNESDAY				
Route:				
Cross Training:				
How I Felt:				

THURSDAY	Weather	Time	Distance	Weekly Total

Route:

Cross Training:

How I Felt:

FRIDAY	Weather	Time	Distance	Weekly Total

Route:

Cross Training:

How I Felt:

SATURDAY	Weather	Time	Distance	Weekly Total

Route:

Cross Training:

How I Felt:

SUNDAY	Weather	Time	Distance	Weekly Total

Route:

Cross Training:

How I Felt:

Week 26 Wrap Up

Did I meet my goals for the week?   ☐ Yes   ☐ No

What helped me reach my goals or what kept me from reaching my goals:

_____

_____

_____

How do I feel about that? _____

_____

_____

What will I change next week? _____

_____

_____

What will I not change next week? _____

_____

_____

Notes/Other Observations: _____

_____

_____

_____

_____

Congratulations! You've Completed 6 Months.   **Total Miles to Date This Year:** _____

*"I started running around my 30th birthday. I wanted
to lose weight; I didn't anticipate the serenity.
Being in motion, suddenly my body was busy and
so my head could work out some issues I had
swept under a carpet of wine and cheese.
Good therapy, that's a good run."*

Michael Weatherly

Week of ___/___/_____ - ___/___/_____

Goals for Week: _____

_____

_____

MONDAY	Weather	Time	Distance	Weekly Total
Route:				
Cross Training:				
How I Felt:				

TUESDAY	Weather	Time	Distance	Weekly Total
Route:				
Cross Training:				
How I Felt:				

WEDNESDAY	Weather	Time	Distance	Weekly Total
Route:				
Cross Training:				
How I Felt:				

THURSDAY	Weather	Time	Distance	Weekly Total

Route:

Cross Training:

How I Felt:

FRIDAY	Weather	Time	Distance	Weekly Total

Route:

Cross Training:

How I Felt:

SATURDAY	Weather	Time	Distance	Weekly Total

Route:

Cross Training:

How I Felt:

SUNDAY	Weather	Time	Distance	Weekly Total

Route:

Cross Training:

How I Felt:

Week 27 Wrap Up

Did I meet my goals for the week?   ☐ Yes   ☐ No

What helped me reach my goals or what kept me from reaching my goals:

_____

_____

_____

How do I feel about that? _____

_____

_____

What will I change next week? _____

_____

_____

What will I not change next week? _____

_____

_____

Notes/Other Observations: _____

_____

_____

_____

_____

Total Miles to Date This Year: _____

"We run to undo the damage we've done to body and spirit. We run to find some part of ourselves yet undiscovered."

John Bingham

Week of ___/ ___/ _____ - ___/ ___/ _____

Goals for Week: _____

_____

_____

MONDAY	Weather	Time	Distance	Weekly Total
Route:				
Cross Training:				
How I Felt:				

TUESDAY	Weather	Time	Distance	Weekly Total
Route:				
Cross Training:				
How I Felt:				

WEDNESDAY	Weather	Time	Distance	Weekly Total
Route:				
Cross Training:				
How I Felt:				

THURSDAY	Weather	Time	Distance	Weekly Total
Route:				
Cross Training:				
How I Felt:				

FRIDAY	Weather	Time	Distance	Weekly Total
Route:				
Cross Training:				
How I Felt:				

SATURDAY	Weather	Time	Distance	Weekly Total
Route:				
Cross Training:				
How I Felt:				

SUNDAY	Weather	Time	Distance	Weekly Total
Route:				
Cross Training:				
How I Felt:				

Week 28 Wrap Up

Did I meet my goals for the week?   □ Yes   □ No

What helped me reach my goals or what kept me from reaching my goals:

_____

_____

_____

How do I feel about that? _____

_____

_____

What will I change next week? _____

_____

_____

What will I not change next week? _____

_____

_____

Notes/Other Observations: _____

_____

_____

_____

_____

Total Miles to Date This Year: _____

"No one is born a perfect runner. And none of us will become one. But through incremental steps, we can become better runners. And that's the beauty of our sport: There are no shortcuts, nothing is given to us; we earn every mile, and we earn every result."

Pete Magill

Week of ___/___/_____ - ___/___/_____

Goals for Week: _____

_____

_____

MONDAY	Weather	Time	Distance	Weekly Total
Route:				
Cross Training:				
How I Felt:				

TUESDAY	Weather	Time	Distance	Weekly Total
Route:				
Cross Training:				
How I Felt:				

WEDNESDAY	Weather	Time	Distance	Weekly Total
Route:				
Cross Training:				
How I Felt:				

THURSDAY	Weather	Time	Distance	Weekly Total

Route:

Cross Training:

How I Felt:

FRIDAY	Weather	Time	Distance	Weekly Total

Route:

Cross Training:

How I Felt:

SATURDAY	Weather	Time	Distance	Weekly Total

Route:

Cross Training:

How I Felt:

SUNDAY	Weather	Time	Distance	Weekly Total

Route:

Cross Training:

How I Felt:

Week 29 Wrap Up

Did I meet my goals for the week?   □ Yes   □ No

What helped me reach my goals or what kept me from reaching my goals:

_____

_____

_____

How do I feel about that? _____

_____

_____

What will I change next week? _____

_____

_____

What will I not change next week? _____

_____

_____

Notes/Other Observations: _____

_____

_____

_____

_____

Total Miles to Date This Year: _____

"If you become restless, speed up. If you become winded, slow down. You climb the mountain in an equilibrium between restlessness and exhaustion."

Robert Pirsig

Week of ___/___/_____ - ___/___/_____

Goals for Week: _____

_____

_____

MONDAY	Weather	Time	Distance	Weekly Total
Route:				
Cross Training:				
How I Felt:				

TUESDAY	Weather	Time	Distance	Weekly Total
Route:				
Cross Training:				
How I Felt:				

WEDNESDAY	Weather	Time	Distance	Weekly Total
Route:				
Cross Training:				
How I Felt:				

THURSDAY	Weather	Time	Distance	Weekly Total

Route:

Cross Training:

How I Felt:

FRIDAY	Weather	Time	Distance	Weekly Total

Route:

Cross Training:

How I Felt:

SATURDAY	Weather	Time	Distance	Weekly Total

Route:

Cross Training:

How I Felt:

SUNDAY	Weather	Time	Distance	Weekly Total

Route:

Cross Training:

How I Felt:

Week 30 Wrap Up

Did I meet my goals for the week? ☐ Yes ☐ No

What helped me reach my goals or what kept me from reaching my goals:

_____

_____

_____

How do I feel about that? _____

_____

_____

What will I change next week? _____

_____

_____

What will I not change next week? _____

_____

_____

Notes/Other Observations: _____

_____

_____

_____

_____

Total Miles to Date This Year: _____

The white space on this page is suitable for notes if needed.

> *"A course never quite looks the same way twice.*
> *The combinations of weather, season, light, feelings*
> *and thoughts that you find there are ever-changing."*
>
> **Joe Henderson**

Week of ___/___/_____ - ___/___/_____

Goals for Week: _____

_____

_____

MONDAY	Weather	Time	Distance	Weekly Total
Route:				
Cross Training:				
How I Felt:				

TUESDAY	Weather	Time	Distance	Weekly Total
Route:				
Cross Training:				
How I Felt:				

WEDNESDAY	Weather	Time	Distance	Weekly Total
Route:				
Cross Training:				
How I Felt:				

THURSDAY	Weather	Time	Distance	Weekly Total

Route:

Cross Training:

How I Felt:

FRIDAY	Weather	Time	Distance	Weekly Total

Route:

Cross Training:

How I Felt:

SATURDAY	Weather	Time	Distance	Weekly Total

Route:

Cross Training:

How I Felt:

SUNDAY	Weather	Time	Distance	Weekly Total

Route:

Cross Training:

How I Felt:

Week 31 Wrap Up

Did I meet my goals for the week?   ☐ Yes   ☐ No

What helped me reach my goals or what kept me from reaching my goals:

_____

_____

_____

How do I feel about that? _____

_____

_____

What will I change next week? _____

_____

_____

What will I not change next week? _____

_____

_____

Notes/Other Observations: _____

_____

_____

_____

_____

Total Miles to Date This Year: _____

"If one can stick to training throughout many long years, then willpower is no longer a problem. It's raining? That doesn't matter. I'm tired? That's beside the point. It's simply that I have to."

Emil Zatopek

Week of ___/___/_____ - ___/___/_____

Goals for Week: _____

_____

_____

MONDAY	Weather	Time	Distance	Weekly Total

Route:

Cross Training:

How I Felt:

TUESDAY	Weather	Time	Distance	Weekly Total

Route:

Cross Training:

How I Felt:

WEDNESDAY	Weather	Time	Distance	Weekly Total

Route:

Cross Training:

How I Felt:

THURSDAY	Weather	Time	Distance	Weekly Total

Route:

Cross Training:

How I Felt:

FRIDAY	Weather	Time	Distance	Weekly Total

Route:

Cross Training:

How I Felt:

SATURDAY	Weather	Time	Distance	Weekly Total

Route:

Cross Training:

How I Felt:

SUNDAY	Weather	Time	Distance	Weekly Total

Route:

Cross Training:

How I Felt:

Week 32 Wrap Up

Did I meet my goals for the week? ☐ Yes ☐ No

What helped me reach my goals or what kept me from reaching my goals:

_____

_____

_____

How do I feel about that? _____

_____

_____

What will I change next week? _____

_____

_____

What will I not change next week? _____

_____

_____

Notes/Other Observations: _____

_____

_____

_____

_____

Total Miles to Date This Year: _____

"If you train your mind for running,
everything else will be easy."

Amby Burfoot

Week of ___/___/_____ - ___/___/_____

Goals for Week: _____

_____

_____

MONDAY	Weather	Time	Distance	Weekly Total
Route:				
Cross Training:				
How I Felt:				

TUESDAY	Weather	Time	Distance	Weekly Total
Route:				
Cross Training:				
How I Felt:				

WEDNESDAY	Weather	Time	Distance	Weekly Total
Route:				
Cross Training:				
How I Felt:				

THURSDAY	Weather	Time	Distance	Weekly Total

Route:

Cross Training:

How I Felt:

FRIDAY	Weather	Time	Distance	Weekly Total

Route:

Cross Training:

How I Felt:

SATURDAY	Weather	Time	Distance	Weekly Total

Route:

Cross Training:

How I Felt:

SUNDAY	Weather	Time	Distance	Weekly Total

Route:

Cross Training:

How I Felt:

Week 33 Wrap Up

Did I meet my goals for the week?   ☐ Yes   ☐ No

What helped me reach my goals or what kept me from reaching my goals:

_____

_____

_____

How do I feel about that? _____

_____

_____

What will I change next week? _____

_____

_____

What will I not change next week? _____

_____

_____

Notes/Other Observations: _____

_____

_____

_____

Total Miles to Date This Year: _____

"When running, let your jaw hang loose,
don't bunch up your shoulders close to your ears,
and occasionally shake out your hands and arms
to stay relaxed."

Dave Martin, Ph.D.

Week of ___/___/_____ - ___/___/_____

Goals for Week: _____

_____

_____

MONDAY	Weather	Time	Distance	Weekly Total
Route:				
Cross Training:				
How I Felt:				

TUESDAY	Weather	Time	Distance	Weekly Total
Route:				
Cross Training:				
How I Felt:				

WEDNESDAY	Weather	Time	Distance	Weekly Total
Route:				
Cross Training:				
How I Felt:				

THURSDAY	Weather	Time	Distance	Weekly Total

Route:

Cross Training:

How I Felt:

FRIDAY	Weather	Time	Distance	Weekly Total

Route:

Cross Training:

How I Felt:

SATURDAY	Weather	Time	Distance	Weekly Total

Route:

Cross Training:

How I Felt:

SUNDAY	Weather	Time	Distance	Weekly Total

Route:

Cross Training:

How I Felt:

Week 34 Wrap Up

Did I meet my goals for the week?   ☐ Yes   ☐ No

What helped me reach my goals or what kept me from reaching my goals:

_____

_____

_____

How do I feel about that? _____

_____

_____

What will I change next week? _____

_____

_____

What will I not change next week? _____

_____

_____

Notes/Other Observations: _____

_____

_____

_____

_____

Total Miles to Date This Year: _____

The white space on this page is suitable for notes if needed.

"Your body is always trying to tell you where you are.
Beware when you become tired and listless, when you
lose interest in workouts and approach them as
a chore rather than a pleasure."

Dr. George Sheehan

Week of ___/___/_____ - ___/___/_____

Goals for Week: _____

_____

_____

MONDAY	Weather	Time	Distance	Weekly Total

Route:

Cross Training:

How I Felt:

TUESDAY	Weather	Time	Distance	Weekly Total

Route:

Cross Training:

How I Felt:

WEDNESDAY	Weather	Time	Distance	Weekly Total

Route:

Cross Training:

How I Felt:

THURSDAY	Weather	Time	Distance	Weekly Total

Route:

Cross Training:

How I Felt:

FRIDAY	Weather	Time	Distance	Weekly Total

Route:

Cross Training:

How I Felt:

SATURDAY	Weather	Time	Distance	Weekly Total

Route:

Cross Training:

How I Felt:

SUNDAY	Weather	Time	Distance	Weekly Total

Route:

Cross Training:

How I Felt:

Week 35 Wrap Up

Did I meet my goals for the week?   ☐ Yes   ☐ No

What helped me reach my goals or what kept me from reaching my goals:

_____

_____

_____

How do I feel about that? _____

_____

_____

What will I change next week? _____

_____

_____

What will I not change next week? _____

_____

_____

Notes/Other Observations: _____

_____

_____

_____

_____

Total Miles to Date This Year: _____

"I always loved running…it was something you could do by yourself, and under your own power. You could go in any direction, fast or slow as you wanted, fighting the wind if you felt like it, seeking out new sights just on the strength of your feet and the courage of your lungs."

Jesse Owens

Week of ___/___/_____ - ___/___/_____

Goals for Week: _____

_____

_____

	Weather	Time	Distance	Weekly Total
MONDAY				
Route:				
Cross Training:				
How I Felt:				

	Weather	Time	Distance	Weekly Total
TUESDAY				
Route:				
Cross Training:				
How I Felt:				

	Weather	Time	Distance	Weekly Total
WEDNESDAY				
Route:				
Cross Training:				
How I Felt:				

THURSDAY	Weather	Time	Distance	Weekly Total

Route:

Cross Training:

How I Felt:

FRIDAY	Weather	Time	Distance	Weekly Total

Route:

Cross Training:

How I Felt:

SATURDAY	Weather	Time	Distance	Weekly Total

Route:

Cross Training:

How I Felt:

SUNDAY	Weather	Time	Distance	Weekly Total

Route:

Cross Training:

How I Felt:

Week 36 Wrap Up

Did I meet my goals for the week?   ☐ Yes   ☐ No

What helped me reach my goals or what kept me from reaching my goals:

_____

_____

_____

How do I feel about that? _____

_____

_____

What will I change next week? _____

_____

_____

What will I not change next week? _____

_____

_____

Notes/Other Observations: _____

_____

_____

_____

_____

Total Miles to Date This Year: _____

The white space on this page is suitable for notes if needed.

"There is more to failing than picking yourself up out of the dust, brushing off the grime and trudging onward. For every defeat, there is a victory inside waiting to be let out if the runner can get past feeling sorry for himself."

Ron Daws

Week of ___/___/_____ - ___/___/_____

Goals for Week: _____

_____

_____

MONDAY	Weather	Time	Distance	Weekly Total
Route:				
Cross Training:				
How I Felt:				

TUESDAY	Weather	Time	Distance	Weekly Total
Route:				
Cross Training:				
How I Felt:				

WEDNESDAY	Weather	Time	Distance	Weekly Total
Route:				
Cross Training:				
How I Felt:				

THURSDAY	Weather	Time	Distance	Weekly Total

Route:

Cross Training:

How I Felt:

FRIDAY	Weather	Time	Distance	Weekly Total

Route:

Cross Training:

How I Felt:

SATURDAY	Weather	Time	Distance	Weekly Total

Route:

Cross Training:

How I Felt:

SUNDAY	Weather	Time	Distance	Weekly Total

Route:

Cross Training:

How I Felt:

Week 37 Wrap Up

Did I meet my goals for the week?   ☐ Yes   ☐ No

What helped me reach my goals or what kept me from reaching my goals:

_____

_____

_____

How do I feel about that? _____

_____

_____

What will I change next week? _____

_____

_____

What will I not change next week? _____

_____

_____

Notes/Other Observations: _____

_____

_____

_____

_____

Total Miles to Date This Year: _____

The white space on this page is suitable for notes if needed.

"All runners are tough. Everyone has to have a little fire in them, that even in tough times, can't be turned off."

Shalane Flanagan

Week of ___/ ___/ _____ - ___/ ___/ _____

Goals for Week: _____

_____

_____

MONDAY	Weather	Time	Distance	Weekly Total

Route:
Cross Training:
How I Felt:

TUESDAY	Weather	Time	Distance	Weekly Total

Route:
Cross Training:
How I Felt:

WEDNESDAY	Weather	Time	Distance	Weekly Total

Route:
Cross Training:
How I Felt:

THURSDAY	Weather	Time	Distance	Weekly Total

Route:

Cross Training:

How I Felt:

FRIDAY	Weather	Time	Distance	Weekly Total

Route:

Cross Training:

How I Felt:

SATURDAY	Weather	Time	Distance	Weekly Total

Route:

Cross Training:

How I Felt:

SUNDAY	Weather	Time	Distance	Weekly Total

Route:

Cross Training:

How I Felt:

Week 38 Wrap Up

Did I meet my goals for the week?   ☐ Yes   ☐ No

What helped me reach my goals or what kept me from reaching my goals:

_____

_____

_____

How do I feel about that? _____

_____

_____

What will I change next week? _____

_____

_____

What will I not change next week? _____

_____

_____

Notes/Other Observations: _____

_____

_____

_____

_____

Total Miles to Date This Year: _____

v The white space on this page is suitable for notes if needed.

"Don't get frustrated or give up if you've recently upped your training and aren't seeing big results yet. Sometimes, it takes years for training to 'kick' in, but when it does, you'll run like you have a rocket pack strapped to your back. Fight the urge to give up!"

Jeff Gaudette

Week of ___/___/_____ - ___/___/_____

Goals for Week: _____

_____

_____

	Weather	Time	Distance	Weekly Total
MONDAY				
Route:				
Cross Training:				
How I Felt:				

	Weather	Time	Distance	Weekly Total
TUESDAY				
Route:				
Cross Training:				
How I Felt:				

	Weather	Time	Distance	Weekly Total
WEDNESDAY				
Route:				
Cross Training:				
How I Felt:				

THURSDAY	Weather	Time	Distance	Weekly Total

Route:

Cross Training:

How I Felt:

FRIDAY	Weather	Time	Distance	Weekly Total

Route:

Cross Training:

How I Felt:

SATURDAY	Weather	Time	Distance	Weekly Total

Route:

Cross Training:

How I Felt:

SUNDAY	Weather	Time	Distance	Weekly Total

Route:

Cross Training:

How I Felt:

Week 39 Wrap Up

Did I meet my goals for the week?   ☐ Yes   ☐ No

What helped me reach my goals or what kept me from reaching my goals:

_____

_____

_____

How do I feel about that? _____

_____

_____

What will I change next week? _____

_____

_____

What will I not change next week? _____

_____

_____

Notes/Other Observations: _____

_____

_____

_____

_____

¾ of the Way Through the Year, Good Job!   **Total Miles to Date This Year:** _____

*"Running has made being depressed impossible.
If I'm going through something emotional and just
go outside for a run, you can rest assured
I'll come back with clarity."*

Alanis Morissette

Week of ___/___/_____ - ___/___/_____

Goals for Week: _____

_____

_____

MONDAY	Weather	Time	Distance	Weekly Total

Route:

Cross Training:

How I Felt:

TUESDAY	Weather	Time	Distance	Weekly Total

Route:

Cross Training:

How I Felt:

WEDNESDAY	Weather	Time	Distance	Weekly Total

Route:

Cross Training:

How I Felt:

THURSDAY	Weather	Time	Distance	Weekly Total

Route:

Cross Training:

How I Felt:

FRIDAY	Weather	Time	Distance	Weekly Total

Route:

Cross Training:

How I Felt:

SATURDAY	Weather	Time	Distance	Weekly Total

Route:

Cross Training:

How I Felt:

SUNDAY	Weather	Time	Distance	Weekly Total

Route:

Cross Training:

How I Felt:

Week 40 Wrap Up

Did I meet my goals for the week?   ☐ Yes   ☐ No

What helped me reach my goals or what kept me from reaching my goals:

_____

_____

_____

How do I feel about that? _____

_____

_____

What will I change next week? _____

_____

_____

What will I not change next week? _____

_____

_____

Notes/Other Observations: _____

_____

_____

_____

_____

Total Miles to Date This Year: _____

"Remember, your worst run is always 100 percent better than the person who never tries."

Josh Cox

Week of ___/___/_____ - ___/___/_____

Goals for Week: _____

_____

_____

MONDAY	Weather	Time	Distance	Weekly Total

Route:

Cross Training:

How I Felt:

TUESDAY	Weather	Time	Distance	Weekly Total

Route:

Cross Training:

How I Felt:

WEDNESDAY	Weather	Time	Distance	Weekly Total

Route:

Cross Training:

How I Felt:

THURSDAY	Weather	Time	Distance	Weekly Total

Route:

Cross Training:

How I Felt:

FRIDAY	Weather	Time	Distance	Weekly Total

Route:

Cross Training:

How I Felt:

SATURDAY	Weather	Time	Distance	Weekly Total

Route:

Cross Training:

How I Felt:

SUNDAY	Weather	Time	Distance	Weekly Total

Route:

Cross Training:

How I Felt:

Week 41 Wrap Up

Did I meet my goals for the week?   ☐ Yes   ☐ No

What helped me reach my goals or what kept me from reaching my goals:

_____

_____

_____

How do I feel about that? _____

_____

_____

What will I change next week? _____

_____

_____

What will I not change next week? _____

_____

_____

Notes/Other Observations: _____

_____

_____

_____

_____

Total Miles to Date This Year: _____

> *"I make sure I have some really enjoyable training runs,*
> *remembering to 'smell the roses' along the way.*
> *That way I don't become caught up in*
> *the training-is-everything syndrome."*
>
> **Sue Stricklin**

Week of ___/___/_____ - ___/___/_____

Goals for Week: _____

_____

_____

MONDAY	Weather	Time	Distance	Weekly Total
Route:				
Cross Training:				
How I Felt:				

TUESDAY	Weather	Time	Distance	Weekly Total
Route:				
Cross Training:				
How I Felt:				

WEDNESDAY	Weather	Time	Distance	Weekly Total
Route:				
Cross Training:				
How I Felt:				

THURSDAY	Weather	Time	Distance	Weekly Total

Route:
Cross Training:
How I Felt:

FRIDAY	Weather	Time	Distance	Weekly Total

Route:
Cross Training:
How I Felt:

SATURDAY	Weather	Time	Distance	Weekly Total

Route:
Cross Training:
How I Felt:

SUNDAY	Weather	Time	Distance	Weekly Total

Route:
Cross Training:
How I Felt:

Week 42 Wrap Up

Did I meet my goals for the week? ☐ Yes   ☐ No

What helped me reach my goals or what kept me from reaching my goals:

_____

_____

_____

How do I feel about that? _____

_____

_____

What will I change next week? _____

_____

_____

What will I not change next week? _____

_____

_____

Notes/Other Observations: _____

_____

_____

_____

_____

Total Miles to Date This Year: _____

"Stepping outside the comfort zone is the price I pay to find out how good I can be. If I planned on backing off every time running got difficult I would hang up my shoes and take up knitting."

Desiree Davila

Week of ___/___/_____ - ___/___/_____

Goals for Week: _____

_____

_____

MONDAY	Weather	Time	Distance	Weekly Total
Route:				
Cross Training:				
How I Felt:				

TUESDAY	Weather	Time	Distance	Weekly Total
Route:				
Cross Training:				
How I Felt:				

WEDNESDAY	Weather	Time	Distance	Weekly Total
Route:				
Cross Training:				
How I Felt:				

THURSDAY	Weather	Time	Distance	Weekly Total
Route:				
Cross Training:				
How I Felt:				

FRIDAY	Weather	Time	Distance	Weekly Total
Route:				
Cross Training:				
How I Felt:				

SATURDAY	Weather	Time	Distance	Weekly Total
Route:				
Cross Training:				
How I Felt:				

SUNDAY	Weather	Time	Distance	Weekly Total
Route:				
Cross Training:				
How I Felt:				

Week 43 Wrap Up

Did I meet my goals for the week?   ☐ Yes   ☐ No

What helped me reach my goals or what kept me from reaching my goals:

_____

_____

_____

How do I feel about that? _____

_____

_____

What will I change next week? _____

_____

_____

What will I not change next week? _____

_____

_____

Notes/Other Observations: _____

_____

_____

_____

_____

Total Miles to Date This Year: _____

The white space on this page is suitable for notes if needed.

"A run begins the moment you forget you are running."

Adidas commercial

Week of ___/___/_____ - ___/___/_____

Goals for Week: _____

_____

_____

MONDAY	Weather	Time	Distance	Weekly Total
Route:				
Cross Training:				
How I Felt:				

TUESDAY	Weather	Time	Distance	Weekly Total
Route:				
Cross Training:				
How I Felt:				

WEDNESDAY	Weather	Time	Distance	Weekly Total
Route:				
Cross Training:				
How I Felt:				

THURSDAY	Weather	Time	Distance	Weekly Total

Route:

Cross Training:

How I Felt:

FRIDAY	Weather	Time	Distance	Weekly Total

Route:

Cross Training:

How I Felt:

SATURDAY	Weather	Time	Distance	Weekly Total

Route:

Cross Training:

How I Felt:

SUNDAY	Weather	Time	Distance	Weekly Total

Route:

Cross Training:

How I Felt:

Week 44 Wrap Up

Did I meet my goals for the week?   ☐ Yes   ☐ No

What helped me reach my goals or what kept me from reaching my goals:

_____

_____

_____

How do I feel about that? _____

_____

_____

What will I change next week? _____

_____

_____

What will I not change next week? _____

_____

_____

Notes/Other Observations: _____

_____

_____

_____

_____

Total Miles to Date This Year: _____

*"Never mind what others do; do better than yourself,
beat your own record from day to day,
and you are a success."*

William J.H. Boetcker

Week of ___/___/_____ - ___/___/_____

Goals for Week: _____

_____

_____

MONDAY	Weather	Time	Distance	Weekly Total
Route:				
Cross Training:				
How I Felt:				

TUESDAY	Weather	Time	Distance	Weekly Total
Route:				
Cross Training:				
How I Felt:				

WEDNESDAY	Weather	Time	Distance	Weekly Total
Route:				
Cross Training:				
How I Felt:				

THURSDAY	Weather	Time	Distance	Weekly Total

Route:

Cross Training:

How I Felt:

FRIDAY	Weather	Time	Distance	Weekly Total

Route:

Cross Training:

How I Felt:

SATURDAY	Weather	Time	Distance	Weekly Total

Route:

Cross Training:

How I Felt:

SUNDAY	Weather	Time	Distance	Weekly Total

Route:

Cross Training:

How I Felt:

Week 45 Wrap Up

Did I meet my goals for the week?   ☐ Yes   ☐ No

What helped me reach my goals or what kept me from reaching my goals:

_____

_____

_____

How do I feel about that? _____

_____

_____

What will I change next week? _____

_____

_____

What will I not change next week? _____

_____

_____

Notes/Other Observations: _____

_____

_____

_____

_____

Total Miles to Date This Year: _____

"The long run puts the tiger in the cat."

Bill Squires

Week of ___/___/_____ - ___/___/_____

Goals for Week: _____

_____

_____

	Weather	Time	Distance	Weekly Total
MONDAY				
Route:				
Cross Training:				
How I Felt:				

	Weather	Time	Distance	Weekly Total
TUESDAY				
Route:				
Cross Training:				
How I Felt:				

	Weather	Time	Distance	Weekly Total
WEDNESDAY				
Route:				
Cross Training:				
How I Felt:				

THURSDAY	Weather	Time	Distance	Weekly Total

Route:

Cross Training:

How I Felt:

FRIDAY	Weather	Time	Distance	Weekly Total

Route:

Cross Training:

How I Felt:

SATURDAY	Weather	Time	Distance	Weekly Total

Route:

Cross Training:

How I Felt:

SUNDAY	Weather	Time	Distance	Weekly Total

Route:

Cross Training:

How I Felt:

Week 46 Wrap Up

Did I meet my goals for the week?   □ Yes   □ No

What helped me reach my goals or what kept me from reaching my goals:

_____

_____

_____

How do I feel about that? _____

_____

_____

What will I change next week? _____

_____

_____

What will I not change next week? _____

_____

_____

Notes/Other Observations: _____

_____

_____

_____

_____

Total Miles to Date This Year: _____

The white space on this page is suitable for notes if needed..

"Remember, the feeling you get from a good run is far better than the feeling you get from sitting around wishing you were running."

Sarah Condor

Week of ___/___/_____ - ___/___/_____

Goals for Week: _____

_____

_____

MONDAY	Weather	Time	Distance	Weekly Total
Route:				
Cross Training:				
How I Felt:				

TUESDAY	Weather	Time	Distance	Weekly Total
Route:				
Cross Training:				
How I Felt:				

WEDNESDAY	Weather	Time	Distance	Weekly Total
Route:				
Cross Training:				
How I Felt:				

THURSDAY	Weather	Time	Distance	Weekly Total

Route:

Cross Training:

How I Felt:

FRIDAY	Weather	Time	Distance	Weekly Total

Route:

Cross Training:

How I Felt:

SATURDAY	Weather	Time	Distance	Weekly Total

Route:

Cross Training:

How I Felt:

SUNDAY	Weather	Time	Distance	Weekly Total

Route:

Cross Training:

How I Felt:

Week 47 Wrap Up

Did I meet my goals for the week?   ☐ Yes   ☐ No

What helped me reach my goals or what kept me from reaching my goals:

_____

_____

_____

How do I feel about that? _____

_____

_____

What will I change next week? _____

_____

_____

What will I not change next week? _____

_____

_____

Notes/Other Observations: _____

_____

_____

_____

_____

Total Miles to Date This Year: _____

The white space on this page is suitable for notes if needed.

"We all have bad days and bad workouts, when running gets ugly, when split times seem slow, when you wonder why you started. It will pass."

Hal Higdon

Week of ___/___/_____ - ___/___/_____

Goals for Week: _____

_____

_____

MONDAY	Weather	Time	Distance	Weekly Total

Route:

Cross Training:

How I Felt:

TUESDAY	Weather	Time	Distance	Weekly Total

Route:

Cross Training:

How I Felt:

WEDNESDAY	Weather	Time	Distance	Weekly Total

Route:

Cross Training:

How I Felt:

THURSDAY	Weather	Time	Distance	Weekly Total

Route:

Cross Training:

How I Felt:

FRIDAY	Weather	Time	Distance	Weekly Total

Route:

Cross Training:

How I Felt:

SATURDAY	Weather	Time	Distance	Weekly Total

Route:

Cross Training:

How I Felt:

SUNDAY	Weather	Time	Distance	Weekly Total

Route:

Cross Training:

How I Felt:

Week 48 Wrap Up

Did I meet my goals for the week?   ☐ Yes   ☐ No

What helped me reach my goals or what kept me from reaching my goals:

_____

_____

_____

How do I feel about that? _____

_____

_____

What will I change next week? _____

_____

_____

What will I not change next week? _____

_____

_____

Notes/Other Observations: _____

_____

_____

_____

_____

Total Miles to Date This Year: _____

"I run because it's so symbolic of life. You have to drive yourself to overcome the obstacles. You might feel that you can't. But then you find your inner strength, and realize you're capable of so much more than you thought."

Arthur Blank

Week of ___/___/_____ - ___/___/_____

Goals for Week: _____

_____

_____

MONDAY	Weather	Time	Distance	Weekly Total
Route:				
Cross Training:				
How I Felt:				

TUESDAY	Weather	Time	Distance	Weekly Total
Route:				
Cross Training:				
How I Felt:				

WEDNESDAY	Weather	Time	Distance	Weekly Total
Route:				
Cross Training:				
How I Felt:				

THURSDAY	Weather	Time	Distance	Weekly Total

Route:

Cross Training:

How I Felt:

FRIDAY	Weather	Time	Distance	Weekly Total

Route:

Cross Training:

How I Felt:

SATURDAY	Weather	Time	Distance	Weekly Total

Route:

Cross Training:

How I Felt:

SUNDAY	Weather	Time	Distance	Weekly Total

Route:

Cross Training:

How I Felt:

Week 49 Wrap Up

Did I meet my goals for the week?   ☐ Yes   ☐ No

What helped me reach my goals or what kept me from reaching my goals:

_____

_____

_____

How do I feel about that? _____

_____

_____

What will I change next week? _____

_____

_____

What will I not change next week? _____

_____

_____

Notes/Other Observations: _____

_____

_____

_____

_____

This log ends in 3 weeks ... order a new one today.   **Total Miles to Date This Year:** _____

"Running is the greatest metaphor for life,
because you get out of it what you put into it."

Oprah Winfrey

Week of ___/___/_____ - ___/___/_____

Goals for Week: _____

_____

_____

MONDAY	Weather	Time	Distance	Weekly Total
Route:				
Cross Training:				
How I Felt:				

TUESDAY	Weather	Time	Distance	Weekly Total
Route:				
Cross Training:				
How I Felt:				

WEDNESDAY	Weather	Time	Distance	Weekly Total
Route:				
Cross Training:				
How I Felt:				

THURSDAY	Weather	Time	Distance	Weekly Total

Route:

Cross Training:

How I Felt:

FRIDAY	Weather	Time	Distance	Weekly Total

Route:

Cross Training:

How I Felt:

SATURDAY	Weather	Time	Distance	Weekly Total

Route:

Cross Training:

How I Felt:

SUNDAY	Weather	Time	Distance	Weekly Total

Route:

Cross Training:

How I Felt:

Week 50 Wrap Up

Did I meet my goals for the week?   ☐ Yes   ☐ No

What helped me reach my goals or what kept me from reaching my goals:

_____

_____

_____

How do I feel about that? _____

_____

_____

What will I change next week? _____

_____

_____

What will I not change next week? _____

_____

_____

Notes/Other Observations: _____

_____

_____

_____

_____

Total Miles to Date This Year: _____

*"Running has given me the courage to start,
the determination to keep trying, and the
childlike spirit to have fun along the way.
Run often and run long, but never
outrun your joy of running."*

Julie Isphording

Week of ___/___/_____ - ___/___/_____

Goals for Week: _____

_____

_____

MONDAY	Weather	Time	Distance	Weekly Total
Route:				
Cross Training:				
How I Felt:				

TUESDAY	Weather	Time	Distance	Weekly Total
Route:				
Cross Training:				
How I Felt:				

WEDNESDAY	Weather	Time	Distance	Weekly Total
Route:				
Cross Training:				
How I Felt:				

THURSDAY	Weather	Time	Distance	Weekly Total

Route:
Cross Training:
How I Felt:

FRIDAY	Weather	Time	Distance	Weekly Total

Route:
Cross Training:
How I Felt:

SATURDAY	Weather	Time	Distance	Weekly Total

Route:
Cross Training:
How I Felt:

SUNDAY	Weather	Time	Distance	Weekly Total

Route:
Cross Training:
How I Felt:

Week 51 Wrap Up

Did I meet my goals for the week?   ☐ Yes   ☐ No

What helped me reach my goals or what kept me from reaching my goals:

_____

_____

_____

How do I feel about that? _____

_____

_____

What will I change next week? _____

_____

_____

What will I not change next week? _____

_____

_____

Notes/Other Observations: _____

_____

_____

_____

_____

Total Miles to Date This Year: _____

"The challenge in running is not to aim at doing the things no one else has done, but to keep doing things everyone could do - but most never will."

Joe Henderson

Week of ___/___/_____ - ___/___/_____

Goals for Week: _____

_____

_____

MONDAY	Weather	Time	Distance	Weekly Total
Route:				
Cross Training:				
How I Felt:				

TUESDAY	Weather	Time	Distance	Weekly Total
Route:				
Cross Training:				
How I Felt:				

WEDNESDAY	Weather	Time	Distance	Weekly Total
Route:				
Cross Training:				
How I Felt:				

THURSDAY	Weather	Time	Distance	Weekly Total

Route:

Cross Training:

How I Felt:

FRIDAY	Weather	Time	Distance	Weekly Total

Route:

Cross Training:

How I Felt:

SATURDAY	Weather	Time	Distance	Weekly Total

Route:

Cross Training:

How I Felt:

SUNDAY	Weather	Time	Distance	Weekly Total

Route:

Cross Training:

How I Felt:

Week 52 Wrap Up

Did I meet my goals for the week?   ☐ Yes   ☐ No

What helped me reach my goals or what kept me from reaching my goals:

_____

_____

_____

How do I feel about that? _____

_____

_____

What will I change next week? _____

_____

_____

What will I not change next week? _____

_____

_____

Notes/Other Observations: _____

_____

_____

_____

_____

Congratulations! You've Completed a Full Year.   **Total Miles to Date This Year:** _____

It was being a runner that mattered, not how fast or how far I could run. The joy was in the act of running and in the journey, not in the destination.

John Bingham

Race Logs

Keep a record of the races in which you participate, it's a fun habit to get into. And once you have a few logged, you'll enjoy having reminders to refresh your memories of your race history and accomplishments.

NOTE: in the Notes/Other Observations area, consider including your pace. And if you took splits during the race, consider recording those, too.

"The difference between a jogger and a runner is a race-entry blank."

Dr. George Sheehan

"You're running on guts. On fumes. Your muscles twitch. You throw up. You're delirious. But you keep running because there's no way out of this hell you're in, because there's no way you're not crossing the finish line. It's a misery that non-runners don't understand."

Martine Costello

"To me, the real test of one's character isn't defined by completing the marathon on race day, but rather by having the self-discipline and dedication to commit, sacrifice, and endure the months of training required to complete such an event."

Kimberly Pasienza

Race Log

Race Name: _____

Distance: _____ My Personal Best at this Distance: _____

Run in this Race Before? ☐ Yes   ☐ No

If "Yes", What Was My Time: _____

Running   ☐ Alone   ☐ with Friends

Friends Participating: _____

_____

Attitude at Beginning of Race: _____

_____

Attitude at End of Race: _____

_____

Time: _____ Overall Place: _____ Age Division Place: _____

Best Thing about this Race: _____

Worst Thing about this Race: _____

Would I Run this Race Again? ☐ Yes   ☐ No

Why or Why Not? _____

_____

Notes/Other Observations: _____

_____

_____

_____

Race Log

Race Name: _____

Distance: _____ My Personal Best at this Distance: _____

Run in this Race Before? ☐ Yes   ☐ No

If "Yes", What Was My Time: _____

Running   ☐ Alone   ☐ with Friends

Friends Participating: _____

_____

Attitude at Beginning of Race: _____

_____

Attitude at End of Race: _____

_____

Time: _____ Overall Place: _____ Age Division Place: _____

Best Thing about this Race: _____

Worst Thing about this Race: _____

Would I Run this Race Again? ☐ Yes   ☐ No

Why or Why Not? _____

_____

Notes/Other Observations: _____

_____

_____

_____

Race Log

Race Name: _____

Distance: _____ My Personal Best at this Distance: _____

Run in this Race Before? ☐ Yes   ☐ No

If "Yes", What Was My Time: _____

Running   ☐ Alone   ☐ with Friends

Friends Participating: _____

_____

Attitude at Beginning of Race: _____

_____

Attitude at End of Race: _____

_____

Time: _____ Overall Place: _____ Age Division Place: _____

Best Thing about this Race: _____

Worst Thing about this Race: _____

Would I Run this Race Again? ☐ Yes   ☐ No

Why or Why Not? _____

_____

Notes/Other Observations: _____

_____

_____

_____

Race Log

Race Name: _____

Distance: _____ My Personal Best at this Distance: _____

Run in this Race Before? □ Yes   □ No

If "Yes", What Was My Time: _____

Running   □ Alone   □ with Friends

Friends Participating: _____

_____

Attitude at Beginning of Race: _____

_____

Attitude at End of Race: _____

_____

Time: _____ Overall Place: _____ Age Division Place: _____

Best Thing about this Race: _____

Worst Thing about this Race: _____

Would I Run this Race Again? □ Yes   □ No

Why or Why Not? _____

_____

Notes/Other Observations: _____

_____

_____

_____

Race Log

Race Name: _____

Distance: _____ My Personal Best at this Distance: _____

Run in this Race Before? ☐ Yes   ☐ No

If "Yes", What Was My Time: _____

Running   ☐ Alone   ☐ with Friends

Friends Participating: _____

_____

Attitude at Beginning of Race: _____

_____

Attitude at End of Race: _____

_____

Time: _____ Overall Place: _____ Age Division Place: _____

Best Thing about this Race: _____

Worst Thing about this Race: _____

Would I Run this Race Again? ☐ Yes   ☐ No

Why or Why Not? _____

_____

Notes/Other Observations: _____

_____

_____

_____

Race Log

Race Name: _____

Distance: _____ My Personal Best at this Distance: _____

Run in this Race Before? ☐ Yes   ☐ No

If "Yes", What Was My Time: _____

Running   ☐ Alone   ☐ with Friends

Friends Participating: _____

_____

Attitude at Beginning of Race: _____

_____

Attitude at End of Race: _____

_____

Time: _____ Overall Place: _____ Age Division Place: _____

Best Thing about this Race: _____

Worst Thing about this Race: _____

Would I Run this Race Again? ☐ Yes   ☐ No

Why or Why Not? _____

_____

Notes/Other Observations: _____

_____

_____

_____

Race Log

Race Name: _____

Distance: _____ My Personal Best at this Distance: _____

Run in this Race Before? ☐ Yes   ☐ No

If "Yes", What Was My Time: _____

Running   ☐ Alone   ☐ with Friends

Friends Participating: _____

_____

Attitude at Beginning of Race: _____

_____

Attitude at End of Race: _____

_____

Time: _____ Overall Place: _____ Age Division Place: _____

Best Thing about this Race: _____

Worst Thing about this Race: _____

Would I Run this Race Again? ☐ Yes   ☐ No

Why or Why Not? _____

_____

Notes/Other Observations: _____

_____

_____

_____

Race Log

Race Name: _____

Distance: _____ My Personal Best at this Distance: _____

Run in this Race Before? □ Yes   □ No

If "Yes", What Was My Time: _____

Running   □ Alone   □ with Friends

Friends Participating: _____

_____

Attitude at Beginning of Race: _____

_____

Attitude at End of Race: _____

_____

Time: _____ Overall Place: _____ Age Division Place: _____

Best Thing about this Race: _____

Worst Thing about this Race: _____

Would I Run this Race Again? □ Yes   □ No

Why or Why Not? _____

_____

Notes/Other Observations: _____

_____

_____

_____

Race Log

Race Name: _____

Distance: _____ My Personal Best at this Distance: _____

Run in this Race Before? ☐ Yes   ☐ No

If "Yes", What Was My Time: _____

Running   ☐ Alone   ☐ with Friends

Friends Participating: _____

_____

Attitude at Beginning of Race: _____

_____

Attitude at End of Race: _____

_____

Time: _____ Overall Place: _____ Age Division Place: _____

Best Thing about this Race: _____

Worst Thing about this Race: _____

Would I Run this Race Again? ☐ Yes   ☐ No

Why or Why Not? _____

_____

Notes/Other Observations: _____

_____

_____

_____

Race Log

Race Name: _____

Distance: _____ My Personal Best at this Distance: _____

Run in this Race Before? ☐ Yes   ☐ No

If "Yes", What Was My Time: _____

Running   ☐ Alone   ☐ with Friends

Friends Participating: _____

_____

Attitude at Beginning of Race: _____

_____

Attitude at End of Race: _____

_____

Time: _____ Overall Place: _____ Age Division Place: _____

Best Thing about this Race: _____

Worst Thing about this Race: _____

Would I Run this Race Again? ☐ Yes   ☐ No

Why or Why Not? _____

_____

Notes/Other Observations: _____

_____

_____

_____

Race Log

Race Name: _____

Distance: _____ My Personal Best at this Distance: _____

Run in this Race Before? ☐ Yes   ☐ No

If "Yes", What Was My Time: _____

Running   ☐ Alone   ☐ with Friends

Friends Participating: _____

_____

Attitude at Beginning of Race: _____

_____

Attitude at End of Race: _____

_____

Time: _____ Overall Place: _____ Age Division Place: _____

Best Thing about this Race: _____

Worst Thing about this Race: _____

Would I Run this Race Again? ☐ Yes   ☐ No

Why or Why Not? _____

_____

Notes/Other Observations: _____

_____

_____

_____

Race Log

Race Name: _____

Distance: _____ My Personal Best at this Distance: _____

Run in this Race Before? ☐ Yes   ☐ No

If "Yes", What Was My Time: _____

Running   ☐ Alone   ☐ with Friends

Friends Participating: _____

_____

Attitude at Beginning of Race: _____

_____

Attitude at End of Race: _____

_____

Time: _____ Overall Place: _____ Age Division Place: _____

Best Thing about this Race: _____

Worst Thing about this Race: _____

Would I Run this Race Again? ☐ Yes   ☐ No

Why or Why Not? _____

_____

Notes/Other Observations: _____

_____

_____

_____

Race Log

Race Name: _____

Distance: _____ My Personal Best at this Distance: _____

Run in this Race Before? ☐ Yes   ☐ No

If "Yes", What Was My Time: _____

Running   ☐ Alone   ☐ with Friends

Friends Participating: _____

_____

Attitude at Beginning of Race: _____

_____

Attitude at End of Race: _____

_____

Time: _____ Overall Place: _____ Age Division Place: _____

Best Thing about this Race: _____

Worst Thing about this Race: _____

Would I Run this Race Again? ☐ Yes   ☐ No

Why or Why Not? _____

_____

Notes/Other Observations: _____

_____

_____

_____

Race Log

Race Name: _____

Distance: _____ My Personal Best at this Distance: _____

Run in this Race Before? ☐ Yes ☐ No

If "Yes", What Was My Time: _____

Running ☐ Alone ☐ with Friends

Friends Participating: _____

_____

Attitude at Beginning of Race: _____

_____

Attitude at End of Race: _____

_____

Time: _____ Overall Place: _____ Age Division Place: _____

Best Thing about this Race: _____

Worst Thing about this Race: _____

Would I Run this Race Again? ☐ Yes ☐ No

Why or Why Not? _____

_____

Notes/Other Observations: _____

_____

_____

_____

Race Log

Race Name: _____

Distance: _____ My Personal Best at this Distance: _____

Run in this Race Before? ☐ Yes   ☐ No

If "Yes", What Was My Time: _____

Running   ☐ Alone   ☐ with Friends

Friends Participating: _____

_____

Attitude at Beginning of Race: _____

_____

Attitude at End of Race: _____

_____

Time: _____ Overall Place: _____ Age Division Place: _____

Best Thing about this Race: _____

Worst Thing about this Race: _____

Would I Run this Race Again? ☐ Yes   ☐ No

Why or Why Not? _____

_____

Notes/Other Observations: _____

_____

_____

_____

Race Log

Race Name: _____

Distance: _____ My Personal Best at this Distance: _____

Run in this Race Before? ☐ Yes   ☐ No

If "Yes", What Was My Time: _____

Running   ☐ Alone   ☐ with Friends

Friends Participating: _____

_____

Attitude at Beginning of Race: _____

_____

Attitude at End of Race: _____

_____

Time: _____ Overall Place: _____ Age Division Place: _____

Best Thing about this Race: _____

Worst Thing about this Race: _____

Would I Run this Race Again? ☐ Yes   ☐ No

Why or Why Not? _____

_____

Notes/Other Observations: _____

_____

_____

_____

Race Log

Race Name: _____

Distance: _____ My Personal Best at this Distance: _____

Run in this Race Before? ☐ Yes   ☐ No

If "Yes", What Was My Time: _____

Running   ☐ Alone   ☐ with Friends

Friends Participating: _____

_____

Attitude at Beginning of Race: _____

_____

Attitude at End of Race: _____

_____

Time: _____ Overall Place: _____ Age Division Place: _____

Best Thing about this Race: _____

Worst Thing about this Race: _____

Would I Run this Race Again? ☐ Yes   ☐ No

Why or Why Not? _____

_____

Notes/Other Observations: _____

_____

_____

_____

Race Log

Race Name: _____

Distance: _____ My Personal Best at this Distance: _____

Run in this Race Before? □ Yes   □ No

If "Yes", What Was My Time: _____

Running   □ Alone   □ with Friends

Friends Participating: _____

_____

Attitude at Beginning of Race: _____

_____

Attitude at End of Race: _____

_____

Time: _____ Overall Place: _____ Age Division Place: _____

Best Thing about this Race: _____

Worst Thing about this Race: _____

Would I Run this Race Again? □ Yes   □ No

Why or Why Not? _____

_____

Notes/Other Observations: _____

_____

_____

_____

Race Log

Race Name: _____

Distance: _____ My Personal Best at this Distance: _____

Run in this Race Before? ☐ Yes   ☐ No

If "Yes", What Was My Time: _____

Running   ☐ Alone   ☐ with Friends

Friends Participating: _____

_____

Attitude at Beginning of Race: _____

_____

Attitude at End of Race: _____

_____

Time: _____ Overall Place: _____ Age Division Place: _____

Best Thing about this Race: _____

Worst Thing about this Race: _____

Would I Run this Race Again? ☐ Yes   ☐ No

Why or Why Not? _____

_____

Notes/Other Observations: _____

_____

_____

_____

Race Log

Race Name: _____

Distance: _____ My Personal Best at this Distance: _____

Run in this Race Before? ☐ Yes ☐ No

If "Yes", What Was My Time: _____

Running ☐ Alone ☐ with Friends

Friends Participating: _____

_____

Attitude at Beginning of Race: _____

_____

Attitude at End of Race: _____

_____

Time: _____ Overall Place: _____ Age Division Place: _____

Best Thing about this Race: _____

Worst Thing about this Race: _____

Would I Run this Race Again? ☐ Yes ☐ No

Why or Why Not? _____

_____

Notes/Other Observations: _____

_____

_____

_____

Race Log

Race Name: _____

Distance: _____ My Personal Best at this Distance: _____

Run in this Race Before? ☐ Yes   ☐ No

If "Yes", What Was My Time: _____

Running   ☐ Alone   ☐ with Friends

Friends Participating: _____

_____

Attitude at Beginning of Race: _____

_____

Attitude at End of Race: _____

_____

Time: _____ Overall Place: _____ Age Division Place: _____

Best Thing about this Race: _____

Worst Thing about this Race: _____

Would I Run this Race Again? ☐ Yes   ☐ No

Why or Why Not? _____

_____

Notes/Other Observations: _____

_____

_____

_____

Race Log

Race Name: _____

Distance: _____ My Personal Best at this Distance: _____

Run in this Race Before? ☐ Yes   ☐ No

If "Yes", What Was My Time: _____

Running   ☐ Alone   ☐ with Friends

Friends Participating: _____

_____

Attitude at Beginning of Race: _____

_____

Attitude at End of Race: _____

_____

Time: _____ Overall Place: _____ Age Division Place: _____

Best Thing about this Race: _____

Worst Thing about this Race: _____

Would I Run this Race Again? ☐ Yes   ☐ No

Why or Why Not? _____

_____

Notes/Other Observations: _____

_____

_____

_____

Race Log

Race Name: _____

Distance: _____ My Personal Best at this Distance: _____

Run in this Race Before? □ Yes   □ No

If "Yes", What Was My Time: _____

Running   □ Alone   □ with Friends

Friends Participating: _____

_____

Attitude at Beginning of Race: _____

_____

Attitude at End of Race: _____

_____

Time: _____ Overall Place: _____ Age Division Place: _____

Best Thing about this Race: _____

Worst Thing about this Race: _____

Would I Run this Race Again? □ Yes   □ No

Why or Why Not? _____

_____

Notes/Other Observations: _____

_____

_____

_____

Race Log

Race Name: _____

Distance: _____ My Personal Best at this Distance: _____

Run in this Race Before? ☐ Yes   ☐ No

If "Yes", What Was My Time: _____

Running   ☐ Alone   ☐ with Friends

Friends Participating: _____

_____

Attitude at Beginning of Race: _____

_____

Attitude at End of Race: _____

_____

Time: _____ Overall Place: _____ Age Division Place: _____

Best Thing about this Race: _____

Worst Thing about this Race: _____

Would I Run this Race Again? ☐ Yes   ☐ No

Why or Why Not? _____

_____

Notes/Other Observations: _____

_____

_____

_____

"Running has given me the courage to start,
the determination to keep trying, and
the childlike spirit to have fun along the way.
Run often and run long, but
never outrun your joy of running."

Julie Isphording

Footwear Log

First Wear Date	Brand	Model	Size	Last Wear Date	Total Mileage
Notes:					
Notes:					
Notes:					
Notes:					
Notes:					
Notes:					
Notes:					
Notes:					

" A good pair of running shoes should last you 400 to 500 miles and is one of the most critical purchases you will make." **John Hanc**

Footwear Log

First Wear Date	Brand	Model	Size	Last Wear Date	Total Mileage
Notes:					
Notes:					
Notes:					
Notes:					
Notes:					
Notes:					
Notes:					
Notes:					

"I double-knot my shoe laces. It's a pain untying your shoes afterward – particularly if you get them wet -- but so is stopping in the middle of a race to tie them." **Hal Higdon**

The Perceptive Runner

Here is one of the inspirational stories from the book "Olympic Spirit" by R. Scott Frothingham, available at amazon.com and other retailers.

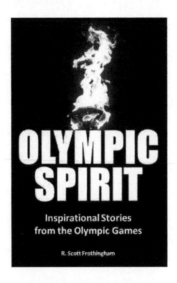

The Perceptive Runner

When Mongolian Pyambu Tuul started the marathon at the 1992 Barcelona Olympics, he was not expected to win a medal. And he performed as expected, falling back to the rear of the pack soon after the start of Games' most grueling event.

When Hwang Young-cho of Korea crossed after the line in 2 hours 13 minutes and 23 seconds to win the Gold medal, Tuul still was about two hours away from the stadium.

When he came in last, finishing the race a couple of minutes over four hours, a reporter asked him why he was so slow and he replied "'No, my time was not slow, after all you could call my run a Mongolian Olympic marathon record."

Then another reporter asked him whether it was the greatest day of his life and Tuul humbly offered this stunning response:

"And as for it being the greatest day of my life, no it isn't", he said, "Up till six months ago I had no sight at all. I was a totally blind person. When I trained it was only with the aid of friends who ran with me. But a group of doctors came to my country last year to do humanitarian medical work. One doctor took a look at my eyes and asked me questions. I told him I had been unable to see since childhood. He said 'But I can fix your sight with a simple operation'. So he did the operation on me and after 20 years I could see again. So today wasn't the greatest day of my life. The best day was when I got my sight back and I saw my wife and two daughters for the first time. And they are beautiful."

Recommendations

Here are 5 quotes from Olympic Medal winners (selected from the 140+ quotes in the book "Olympic Gold" available on amazon.com and from other retailers).

"The greatest memory for me of the 1984 Olympics was not the individual honors, but standing on the podium with my teammates to receive our team gold medal." - Mitch Gaylord, 4 time Olympic medalist - gymnastics

"I didn't set out to beat the world; I just set out to do my absolute best." -Al Oerter, 4 time Olympic medalist - track and field

"It is the inspiration of the Olympic Games that drives people not only to compete but to improve, and to bring lasting spiritual and moral benefits to the athlete and inspiration to those lucky enough to witness the athletic dedication." - Herb Elliott, 1 time Olympic medalist - track and field

"We all have dreams. But in order to make dreams come into reality, it takes an awful lot of determination, dedication, self-discipline, and effort." -Jesse Owens, 4 time Olympic medalist - track and field

"At the two-thirds mark, I think of those who are still with me. Who might break? Should I? Then I give it all I've got." -Ibrahim Hussein, 2 Olympic Games- track and field

Also available from amazon.com and other retailers:

Running isn't a sport for pretty boys...
It's about the sweat in your hair and the blisters on your feet.
Its the frozen spit on your chin and the nausea in your gut.
It's about throbbing calves and cramps at midnight that
are strong enough to wake the dead.
It's about getting out the door and running
when the rest of the world is only dreaming about
having the passion that you need to
live each and every day with.
It's about being on a lonely road and running like
a champion even when there's not a single soul
in sight to cheer you on.
Running is all about having the desire to train and
persevere until every fiber in your legs, mind,
and heart is turned to steel.
And when you've finally forged hard enough,
you will have become the best runner you can be.
And that's all that you can ask for.

Paul Maurer

May your miles be many
and your injuries few.
Here's to PBs a plenty --
a life of amazing runs for you.

Sebastian

FastForwardPublishing.com

Printed in Great Britain
by Amazon